HOW DO YOUR MUSCLES MOVE?

Written by John Farndon
Illustrated by Alan Rowe

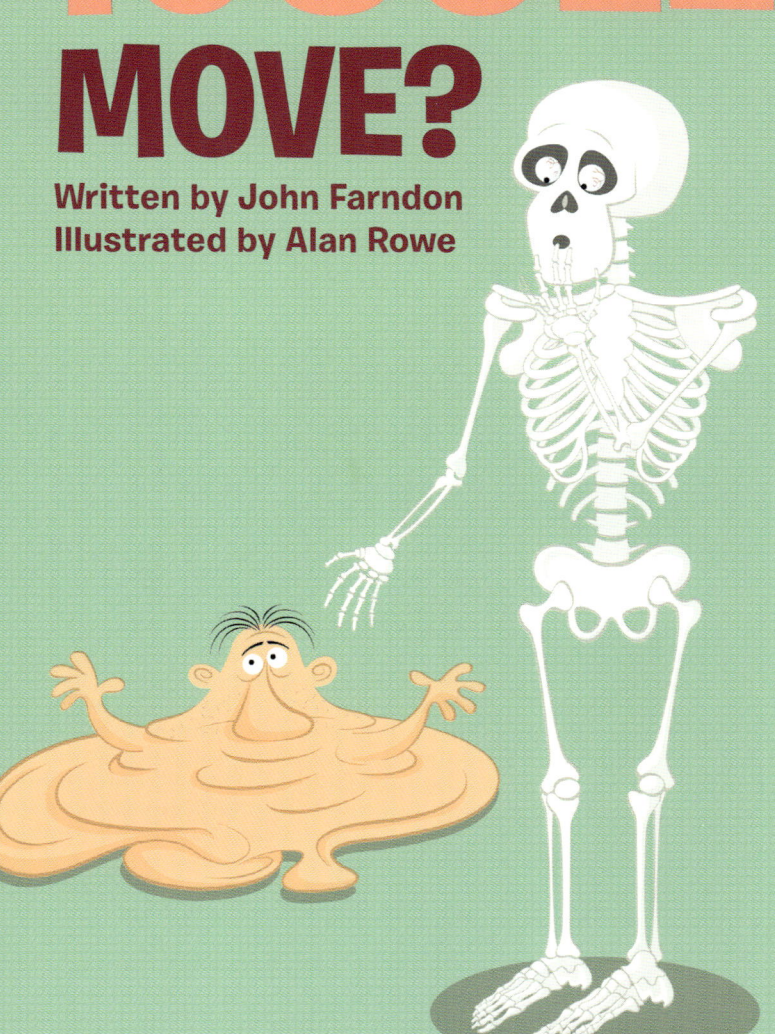

Copyright © 2022 Hungry Tomato Ltd

First published in 2022 by Hungry Tomato Ltd
F15, Old Bakery Studios, Blewetts Wharf, Malpas Road, Truro, Cornwall, TR1 1QH, UK.

No part of this publication may be reproduced, stored in a retrieval system, or transmitted in any form or by any means, electronic, mechanical, photocopying, recording, or otherwise, without prior written permission of the copyright owner.

A CIP catalog record for this book is available from the British Library.

ISBN 978-1-915461-07-0

Manufactured in the USA

Discover more at
www.hungrytomato.com

CONTENTS

HOW DO YOUR MUSCLES MOVE?	4
MIGHTY MUSCLES	6
BUILDING STRENGTH	8
YOUR BONY FRAME	10
JOINING TOGETHER	12
SKIN DEEP	14
SWEATY, OILY SKIN	16
GROWING PARTS	18
CUTS AND BRUISES	20
GLOSSARY	22
INDEX	23

HOW DO YOUR MUSCLES MOVE?

Your body is an incredible machine that can do all sorts of awesome things. Have you ever thought about where your strength comes from or how you move your body?

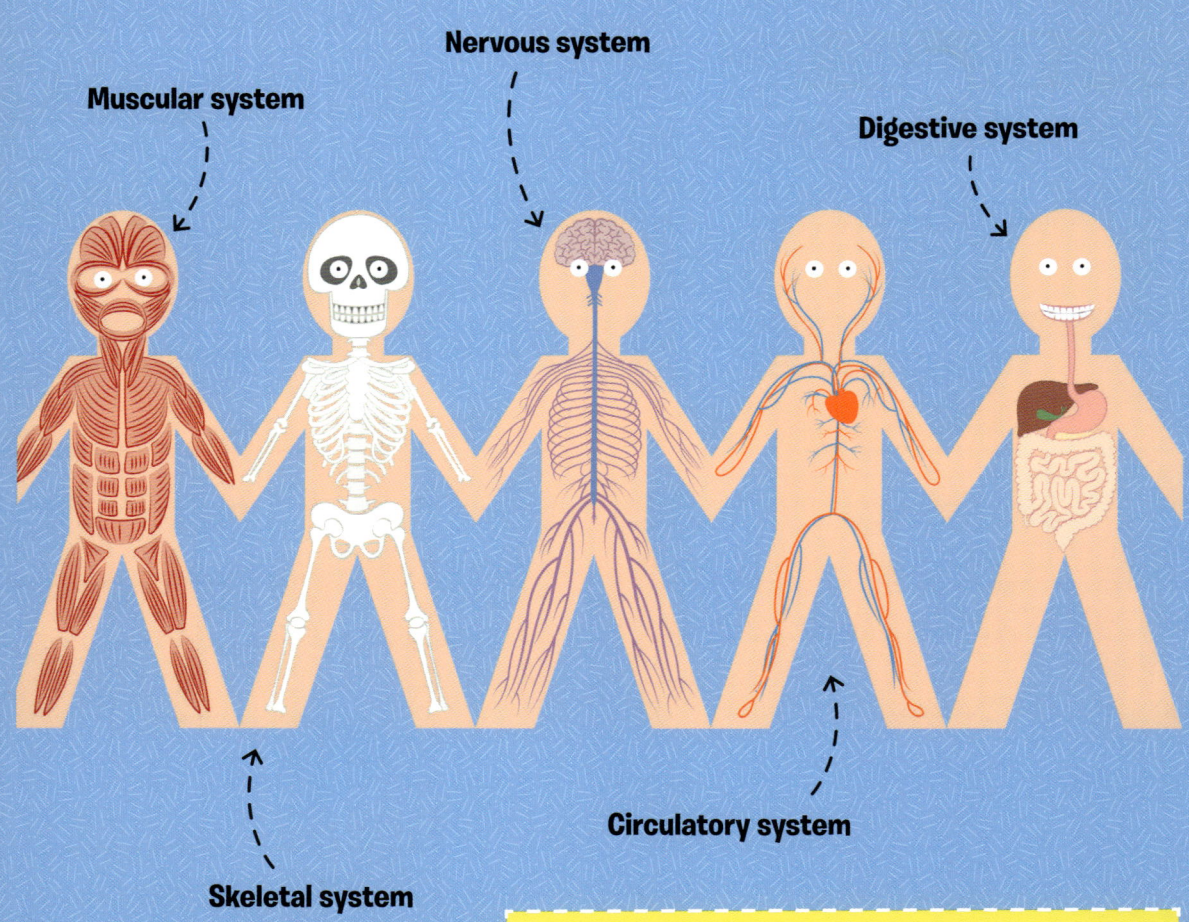

Muscular system

Nervous system

Digestive system

Skeletal system

Circulatory system

How does your body work?

Your body is all about teamwork. Different parts work together in teams, called systems, to perform different tasks.

What's holding you together?

Your muscular and skeletal systems make your body move and hold everything in place, while your skin forms a protective outer layer.

Let's find out more about your amazing muscles, bones and skin.

MIGHTY MUSCLES
If you just turned the page, then your muscles helped you do it. But how?

What are muscles?
Muscles are bundles of rope-like **tissue**. They do just one simple thing, get shorter!

Where have you got muscles?
You've got more than 650 muscles all over your body. Here are a few of them:

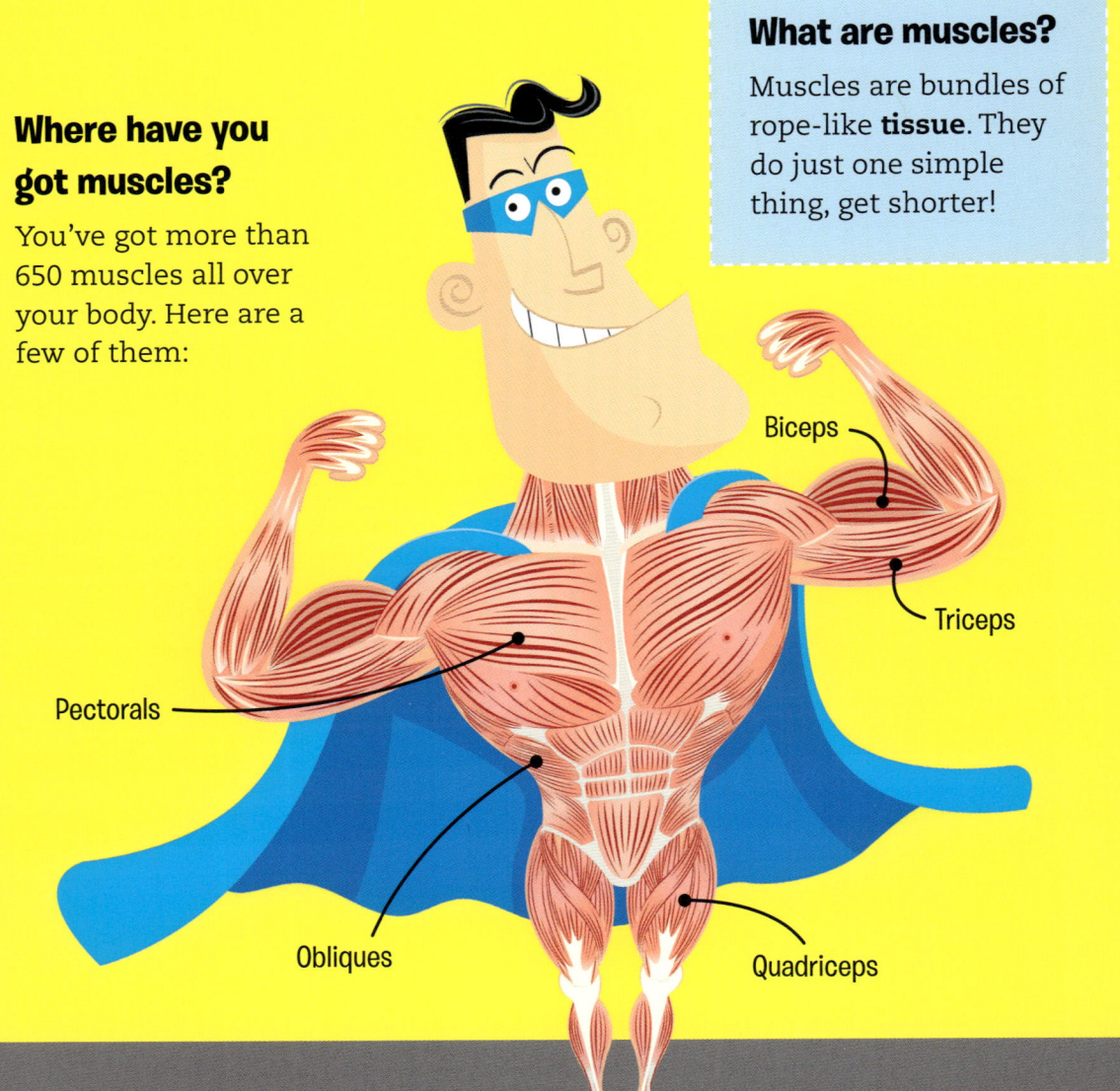

- Biceps
- Triceps
- Pectorals
- Obliques
- Quadriceps

Pulls to straighten leg

Pulls to bend leg

How do muscles pull and push?

Muscles can only pull to get shorter. That's why they come in pairs: one to pull (called the flexor) and the other to pull it back (the extensor).

Biceps
The biceps muscle in your upper arm lifts your hand.

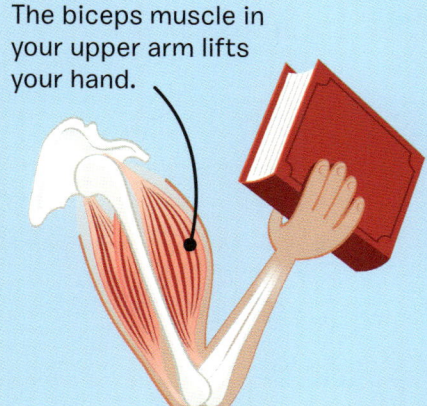

Triceps
The triceps muscle in your upper arm lets it down.

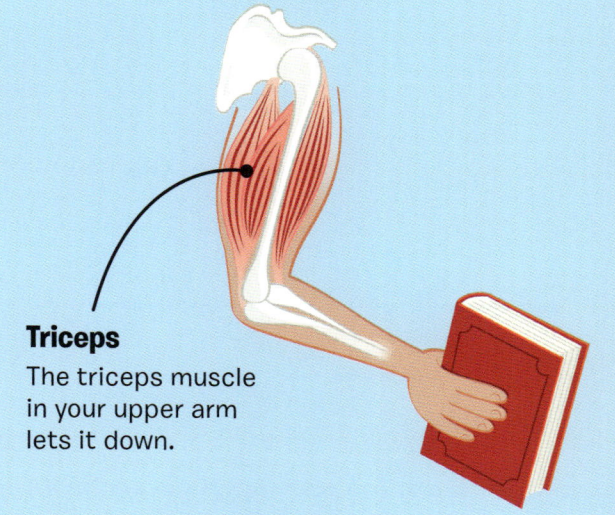

How do you move your hand?

When you picked up this book, your brain told the right muscles to pull, and your hand moved. Amazing!

7

BUILDING STRENGTH

Your muscles make you strong. Without them, you couldn't lift, pull or push things.

Why do athletes need to train?

Training makes your muscles grow bigger and stronger so they can pull better. If you don't use them regularly, they get smaller and weaker.

How do muscles grow bigger?

When you exercise a lot, the muscle tissue you use starts to get longer and stronger. Then you start to grow more of it.

What's your strongest muscle?

Ever bitten your tongue? Then you'll know! Your strongest muscle is the masseter muscle, which makes your teeth bite together.

(Don't try this at home!)

What's your biggest muscle?

You're sitting on it. Scientists call it the gluteus maximus, but it's really just your butt.

YOUR BONY FRAME

Flesh and muscles are pretty soft and full of water. So what keeps you upright?

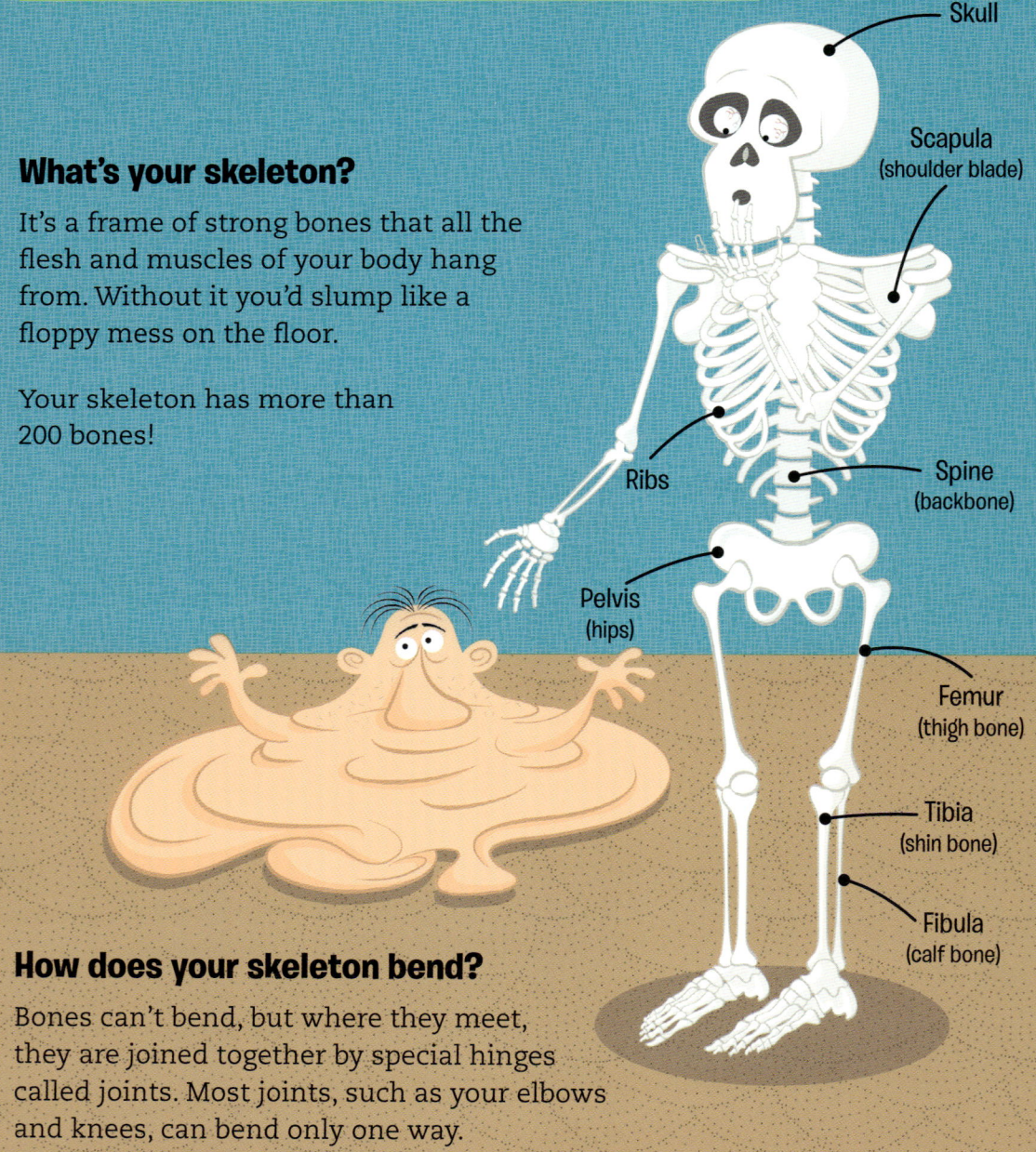

What's your skeleton?

It's a frame of strong bones that all the flesh and muscles of your body hang from. Without it you'd slump like a floppy mess on the floor.

Your skeleton has more than 200 bones!

How does your skeleton bend?

Bones can't bend, but where they meet, they are joined together by special hinges called joints. Most joints, such as your elbows and knees, can bend only one way.

What's your bendiest joint?

In your shoulder joints and hip joints, the arm bones and leg bones end in a ball that sits in a cup. The ball can move in a lot of different directions.

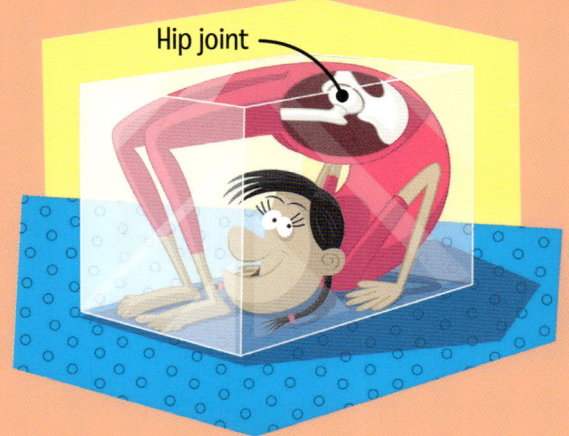

What's inside your bones?

The outside of a bone is solid, but inside it is full of holes like a sponge.

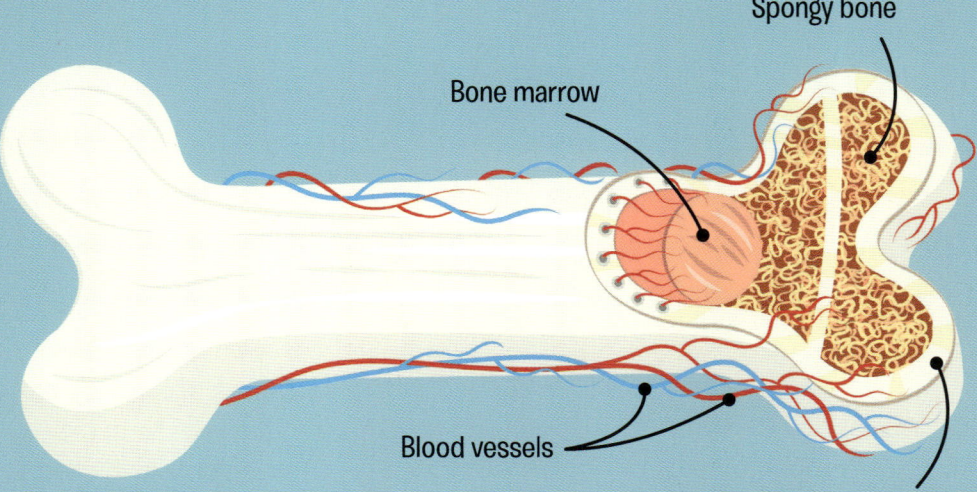

Many of your bones are filled with soft, gel-like stuff, called marrow. Some is red and bloody, and some is yellow and fatty. Red marrow is your body's factory for making red blood **cells**.

JOINING TOGETHER

Your bones come in lots of shapes and sizes, and fit together in different ways. It's like a puzzle!

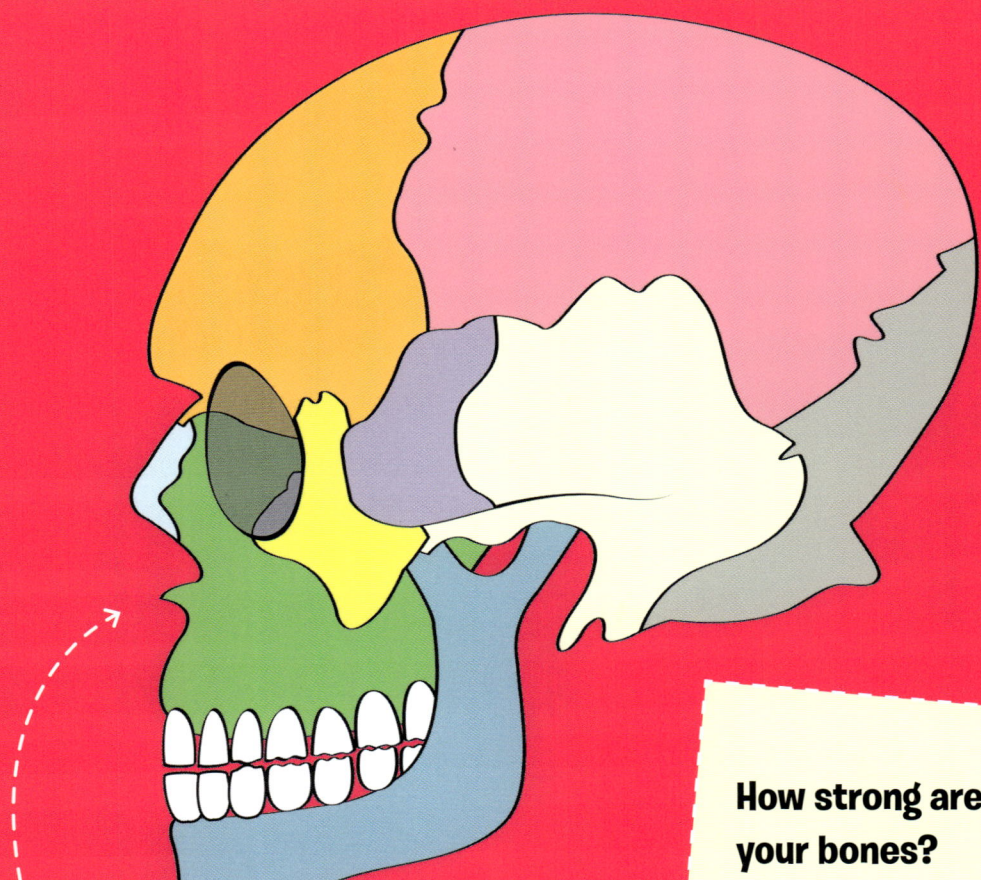

Why is your head hard?

Your precious brain is protected by a hard case of bone called your skull. It is made from 22 pieces, which are all joined firmly together.

How strong are your bones?

For their weight, bones are very strong. They are four times as strong as concrete! They are also very light, because of all the holes inside.

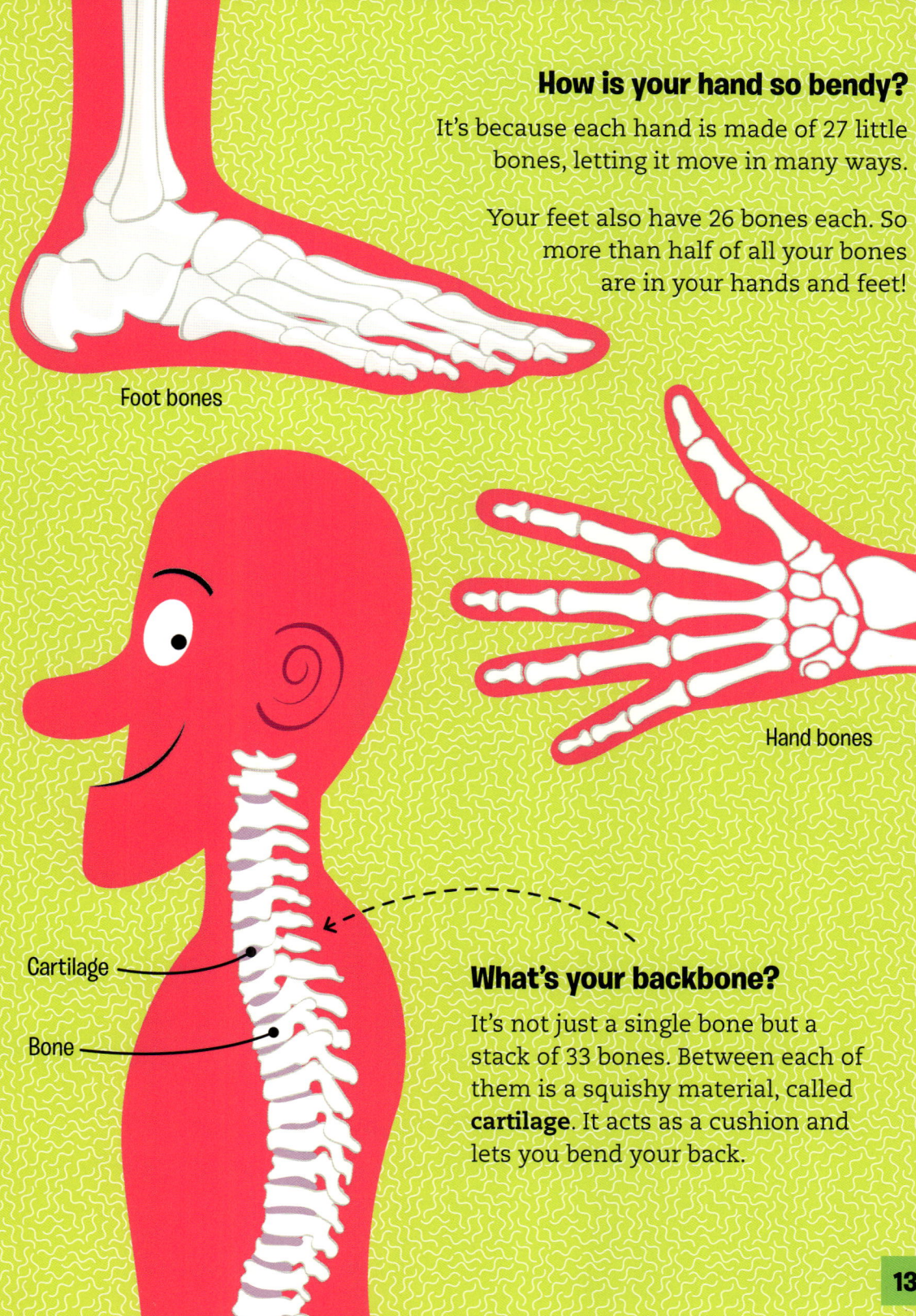

How is your hand so bendy?

It's because each hand is made of 27 little bones, letting it move in many ways.

Your feet also have 26 bones each. So more than half of all your bones are in your hands and feet!

Foot bones

Hand bones

Cartilage

Bone

What's your backbone?

It's not just a single bone but a stack of 33 bones. Between each of them is a squishy material, called **cartilage**. It acts as a cushion and lets you bend your back.

SKIN DEEP

Your body is covered in skin, from head to toe. How much do you know about it?

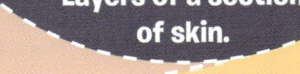

Pores

Hair

Epidermis
The protective outer layer.

Dermis
Where you feel things and where your hair grows.

Subcutaneous fat
This layer keeps you warm.

Layers of a section of skin.

Why do we have skin?

It's your protective suit. It's waterproof, keeps you warm and it's good at keeping out **germs** and dirt (most of the time).

How big is your skin?

Your skin is the heaviest part of your body and weighs 5 to 10 pounds (2–4.5 kg), about the same as a cat. If you rolled it out, it would cover your whole bed.

14

Does your skin ever change?

Your body keeps your skin fresh by adding new cells and shedding old ones. In fact, you replace your whole skin every month. You could lose more than 1,000 skins in your lifetime!

What happens to old skin?

You lose more than 30,000 skin cells every minute. More than half the dust in your house is your old skin!

Tiny creatures called dust mites chomp on it all the time. Eugghh!

SWEATY, OILY SKIN

If your skin gets renewed all the time, shouldn't it stay clean by itself?

Why do you need to bathe?

The sweat, oil and dead cells made by your skin are a lovely home for germs! If you don't wash regularly, you may start to get smelly. Germs can also get in through cuts and make you ill.

WE'RE MOVING IN!

How do you sweat, and why?

Your skin is covered in tiny holes, called pores. One kind oozes oil, called sebum, to keep your skin flexible. The other oozes water (or sweat), which helps your body keep cool.

What's dandruff?

Dandruff is when a lot of little flakes, made of dead skin cells and oil, form on your **scalp**. It can be embarrassing and itchy, but it's very common and easy to treat.

What are zits?

Zits, spots, pimples (whatever you call them), can form when pores get clogged up with dead skin cells, oil and germs.

Some zits turn red and fill with **pus**. It might be tempting to pop them, but don't! It can make things worse.

GROWING PARTS

It's great growing bigger and stronger, isn't it? But which parts of your body just won't stop growing?

Why do you need a haircut?

You should have about 100,000 hairs growing from your head. Hair grows faster than anything else in your body; more than half an inch (13 mm) a month.

How strong is hair?

A rope made from a thousand of your hairs could lift a grown-up. If you used every one of your hairs, it could lift two African elephants!

How fast do nails grow?

Fingernails grow faster than toenails, and your middle one grows fastest of all. Your fingernails would grow almost 100 feet (30 m) long in your lifetime, if you didn't cut them.

Why doesn't cutting nails and hair hurt?

Because they are not alive! They are made of keratin, a material left by dead cells. Only the root is alive and has **nerves** attached, which makes it able to feel.

HELP ME!

Skin

Hair root

CUTS AND BRUISES

It's your skin that takes the damage if you fall or cut yourself. Ouch!

OH NO, NOT AGAIN!

What's a bruise?

If you fall and get a bruise, your skin is bleeding on the inside.

What's a graze?

A graze is when you scrape the surface of the skin. It can be very sore, but doesn't break through the skin.

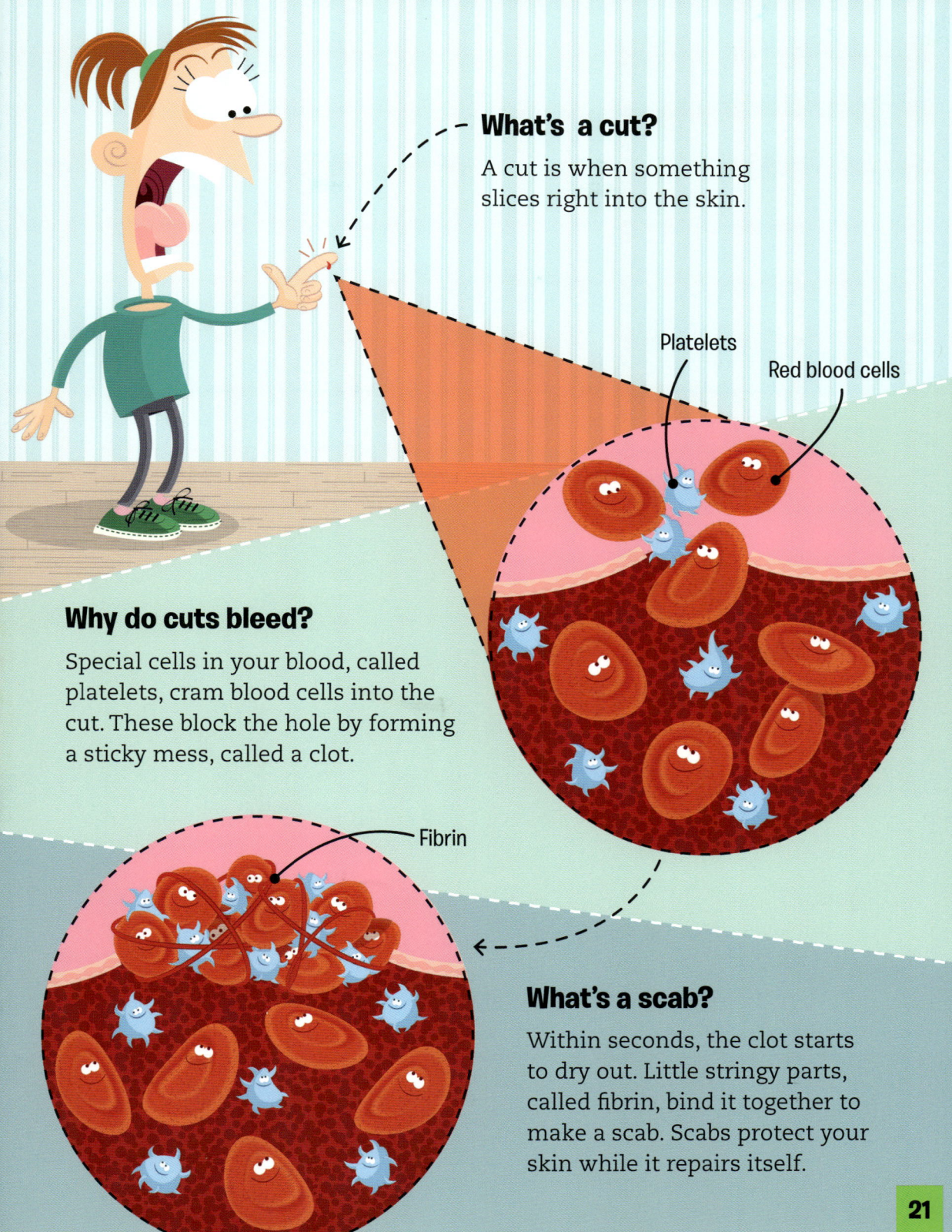

GLOSSARY

cartilage
A tough, rubbery material. It makes your nose and ears bendy, and acts like a cushion in your knees.

cells
Our bodies are made up of trillions of tiny, squishy packages, called cells. We have lots of different types of cells for each body part.

germs
Tiny living things, including bacteria and viruses, that can make you ill if they get inside your body.

nerves
Nerves are made of special cells (see above), called neurons, these neurons send messages between the brain and the rest of the body.

pus
A thick yellowish-white fluid that can form in response to an infection.

scalp
The skin on your head, under your hair.

tissue
Similar cells (see opposite) grow together to make tissues, which make up body parts, such as muscles, bones and skin. Connective tissue connects different parts of the body together.

INDEX

B
backbone (spine) 10, 13
blood 11, 21
blood vessels 11
bone marrow 11
bones 5, 10-13
brain 7, 12
bruise 20

C
cartilage 13, 22
cells 11, 15, 16-17, 19, 21, 22
cuts 16, 20-21

D
dandruff 17,
dust mites 16

F
fat 14
foot 13

G
germs 14, 16-17, 22
graze 20

H
hair 14, 18-19
hand 7, 13

J
joints 10-11

M
muscles 4-5, 6-10

N
nails 19
nerves 19, 22

P
platelets 21
pores 16-17
pus 17, 22

R
red blood cell 11, 21

S
scab 21
scalp 17, 22
skeleton 10
skin 5, 14-17, 19-21

skull 10, 12
spine (see backbone)
sweat 16
systems 4-5

T
teeth 9
tongue 9

Z
zits 17

About the Author

John Farndon is the author of a huge number of books for adults and children on science, history and nature, including international bestsellers, *Do Not Open* and *Do You Think You're Clever?*. He has been shortlisted for the Young People's Science Book Prize five times, including for the book *Project Body*.

About the Illustrator

Alan Rowe has been working as a freelance Illustrator since 1985. His work is heavily influenced by 1950s and 60s cartoons. Maybe all that time spent glued to the TV as a child wasn't all wasted!